PIAZZA
ARMERINA
The mosaics and Morgantina

Edited and written by
Padre Carmelo Capizzi S.J.
e Francesco Galati

Published by
ITALCARDS
bologna Italy

Sole distributor for Sicily
Nicolò Maltese
Via Carmelo di Marco, 2 - Tel. 0935/85075
94015 Piazza Armerina (ENNA)

PIAZZA ARMERINA

Piazza Armerina is situated above three rises, and it is flanked by verdant hills and mountains (the Erei). When one comes by the ordinary road, he can reach the town by an excellent set of motorways (when one comes from Catania on autostrada A 19, he takes the exit at Molinello; when he comes from Palermo on the same autostrada, he takes the exit at Enna; there are superstradas from Gela and from Caltagirone). Piazza Armerina is a vivacious, populous and developed urban center in the «Heart of Sicily», which is distinguished by the richness of its springs, gardens and forests. Its mediaeval, renaissance and baroque monuments prevent it from being confused with other towns.

It stands at the center of a quite extensive classical and mediaeval archaeological zone (Montagna di Marzo, Monte Naone, Rossomanno, and Monte Calvano). It arose on its present site in the XIIth century through the efforts of a composite population, which came for the much part from the ancient Aleramic March of Monferrato (whence the gallo-italic dialect still spoken by the townpeople), after a more ancient Piazza — the Arab Iblâtasah — situated in the present district of Casale was destroyed in 1161 by the Norman king William I.

The Cathedral with the surrounding inhabited area seen by night and by day.

It was the favorite residence of crusader knights and above all of the Savonese branch of the Marquesses of Monferrato, who constructed outstanding monuments there (Sant'Andrea, Santa Maria di Patrisanto, San Giovanni di Rodi) and granted it the privilege, shared by the city of Savona of incorporating in the stemma of the city the arms of the «gens Aleramica».

Piazza (the specification «Armerina» only goes back to 1862) was from its very beginning a governmental city, and moreover in the Suevan and Angevin Period it was the seat of the National Court of the «Regnum Siciliae»; and Frederick III of Aragon also convoked there the Parliaments in 1296 and 1309. It was honored by the Hasburg emperor Charles V with the title «Most Opulent and Faithful City», and was for centuries the chief city of a quite extensive «Comarca» or governmental district centering on a town. It was the seat of high judicial magistracies, of an ancient Spiritual Court, and of the Tribunal of the Monarchy. It had, moreover, a University of Studies entrusted to the Jesuits and it had the honor of a citizen Senate. Until 1926 it was the chief city of the surrounding district, and since 1817 it has been the episcopal seat of the diocese of the same name. Public monuments preserve the memory of some of its illustrious sons.

Piazza Armerina has recently acquired international fame thanks to the Roman Villa of the Casale district, a villa to which its quite extensive complex of mosaic pavements give splendor. The

The inside of the cathedral in the form of a latin cross.

A fifteenth century wooden crucifix, work of Antonello da Messina. In the lower part the maker has painted the image of the resurrected Christ.

3

General panorama of Piazza Armerina.

variety of figurative and ornamental motifs, the richness in mythological scenes of daily life and customs, the skill in design, and its chromatic delicacy confer on this monument of the late Roman epoch an inestimable value from both the artistic and historical points of view. The villa, which was constructed somewhere around the IIIrd-IVth centuries after Christ and probably by the emperor Maximianus Herculius, was burned up by a fire which was most probably connected with the destruction of ancient Piazza mentioned above, and it afterwards disappeared by being buried under the mud of a large flood. The Monument, which is considered one of the most important archaelogical discoveries of our time, presents the characteristics of a construction in terraces and is constituted by four architectural units: 1) the principal entrance and the quarter for the baths; 2) the peristyle with living-rooms and guest-rooms; 3) the private apartments and the great basilica; and 4) the tricilium of dining room and the elliptical courtyard.

6

4

6

A visit to the villa is facilitated by a system of walkways resting for the most part on the walls of the perimeter, from which it is possible to admire both close at hand and above the whole grandiose complex of mosaics which have been uncovered so far.

The city also offers the tourist the pleasure of

1. Piazza Garibaldi with the 18th century «Palazzo di città» (City Palace) today site of the town hall. On the right is the 17th century Church of Fundrò dedicated to St. Rocco.
2. The fourteenth century Aragonese Castle, seen by day and by night. It was the residence of King Martin I of Aragon during his reign.
3. A monument to the Fallen of the Great War 1915/18.
4. A 12th century insignia of the Knights of Malta.
5. The 15th century of St. Mary of Jesus.
6. The 12th century Church of St. Andrew.

a walk in its most ancient quarters, whose narrow streets, churches and palaces emanated a charm that sometimes takes one right back into the Middle Ages. A visit to the Piazza Duomo (the highest point of the city: 721 metres or 2,366 feet above sea level) will turn out to be not less fascinating. There one can admire the powerful and harmonious structures of the baroque cathedral, the rather severe front of the Palazzo Trigona, and in the distance the valleys and the surrounding heights. It is also interesting to take a walk in the modern zone for shopping at rather modest prices. Those who like to pass their vacation in a tent or caravan in direct contact with nature can make use of large forested areas (about 2,000 hectars or 4,942 acres) planted with pine, poplar, eucalyptus, cedar, etc. in the immediate neighborood of Piazza Armerina.

Because of its geographical and topographical position, the kindness of its climate, and the tranquillity of its ambient the city lends itself to being a convenient base for excursions into the nearer centers, which have a touristics interest in the widest sense of the word: Aidone with its archaeological museum, its mediaeval edifices, and the quite recent excavations of the Sicilian-Greek city of Morgantina; Caltagirone with its various monuments and its museum of ceramics; Gela and Centuripe with their museum of classical archaeology; the district of Sofiana, Monte Naone and the district of Montagna di Marzo with their remains of urban settlements of the Sicilian, Greek, Roman and Byzantine epochs. Trips to the lakes of the province, to the sea and to the mountains are just as easy: the beach at Gela is less then an hour's distance by auto, while one can reach Etna and the Madonie in less than two hours.

The hotels of the city, which are for the most part quite modern, assure a tranquil and comfortable stay. The cuisine of Piazza Armerina boasts of a special tradition in the area of sweets because of its nougats and its pastries made of almonds. Furthermore, this cuisine, which is rich in excellent national and local dishes, and the relatively light wines of the district are capable of satisfaying the requirements of the most refined connoisseurs.

5

7

SOFIANA

Coming from Gela, one takes the road for Piazza Armerina and at about 5 kms from the town, one turns into a road to the South which, after about 7 kms, reaches the Sofiana exavations, found at 6 kms to the South of the Villa Romana del Casale, being port of the Proedium Philosophianum (as the conserved name and stamped bricks with the writing FILOSOF indicate), then transformed into a Byzantine mass. On the wide spread of the plain which constitutes the district — and on the low hills which crown it are traces of human habitation which, strating from the 8th 7th century B.C. through the Greco-Roman and Byzantine Era reach Norman Times. The excavations have interested a limited part of the centre, recorded in the itinerary of Antonian, as the third last «Statio» of the internal road from Catania to Agrigento. The heating system in view, probably the «Monsio» of the itinerary — is a well conserved structure in certain parts and is dated, through successive modifications, from the 1st to the 4th century A.D., when around it there developed on inhabited area which lasted until the age of Frederick. In the «Calidaris» a Christian Basilica was successively added, furnished with two apses and a baptistry, which can be dated to the end of the 5th century A.D. to a few hundred metres to the South-West of the confines of the inhabited area on a small hill a three naves basilica was built, with apses and a rectangular space in the manner of Narthex; under the floor of the nave, on the left is a fair of large tombs, one of which has seven achromatic vases datable to the 7th century A.D. In the Roman-Byzantine necropolis tens of sepulchres have been excavated (tombs of stones and marble slabs) which have given finds of plates, glass ware, bronzes, vases, amongs which an exemplary is decorated with birds (Museum of Gela).

THE NORMAN PALIO (HISTORICAL HORSE RACE)

It is the most important of all the displays of Piazza, with both a national and international character. It takes place on the 13th and 14th of August every year.

«Preceding Historical and legendary figures»

After the Norman Conquest of South Italy in the early years of the 11th century, the following of investitial of the lands by the Emperor Henry III (1047), the Norman continuity with their conquests, defeated the forces of the Pope Leo IX, at Civitate del Fortore, who missed to curd their advance. In 1059, at the Council held at Melfi, Pope Nicholas II, to avoid ulterior dangers, allied

himself with Robert the Guiscard, to whom he conceded the investiture of the Dukedom of Puglia and Calabria as a Church feud; with the promise of giving him Sicily if he were to succeed in liberating it from the Saracens. Robert, after having swom fealty to the Pope with the other Normans, and after having the Byzantines had occupied Reggio in 1060, began the Holy war of liberation of the island.

Top left: the excavations of Sofiana, show traces of human habitation which, starting from the 8th-7th century B.C. through the Greco-Roman and Byzantine Era reach Norman times.

Costume shows during the Norman Palio (Historical Horse Race) which takes place on the 13th and the 14th of August every year.

After the victory of Cerami (1063) Pope Alexander II sent a banner with the Virgin painted on it to Count Ruggero, as a war banner and as a sign of the investiture and of good wishes for the liberation of Sicily from the Saracen domination.

The Banner, «signum victoriae» carried Ruggero from victory to victory as far as Plutia (Piazza Armerina) which was set up as the Norman Army's drill ground. In this most noble city the troops of the count were gathered and here the Lombard troops who gave up their arms, wanted to remain.

The ancient city of Armerina became a corner store of the Norman conquest and the inhabitants kenw so well how to gain the esteem of Count Ruggero that in 1091, the conquest of Sicily over, he gave the city the banner received from the Pope as a sign of his affection.

THE ROMAN VILLA OF CASALE

Introduction

The aim of this guide of the Roman Villa of Casale is to give tourists information on this famous monument, briefly and schematically, so that they can better value and know what our ancestors left us.

It is a «guide» in the real sense of the word: follow the enclosed map and your visit will be simple, useful and agreeable as well.

FRANCESCO GALATI

Preface

It may seem strange that the Romans, between the IIIrd and the IVth century a.D., built such a wonderful Villa just in the centre of Sicily. But there is a logical explanation, because in that period the Island was divided in large estates and the owner of these large feud probably lived there.

The place was probably different from that we can see now. In fact, west of the built-up area the Gela river flowed and joined the Villa with the town of Gela, and by this way the marbles which adorn the Domus arrived from abroad, since Sicily did not and does not yield precious marbles.

The Villa was built following the shape of the land and it almost lies at the foot of Mount Magone and occupies a surface of about 4,000 sqm.

To understand correctly its structure, we can divide the villa in 3 areas:

1st - There are the *Thermae* or baths;
2nd - There are the guest-rooms;
3^{ed} - There are the rooms of the owner and his family. Besides, there is the large dining-room, the famous Roman triclinium.

Visit to the Villa

After these preliminary remarks, you can visit the monument.

On the left of the entrance there is the Roman acqueduct which reminds us the more imposing work in Rome.

You arrive at the Thermae, in front of the praefurnia (A) with baked-clay pipes; the function of these pipes was to prevent the breaking of the wall when the fire was lighted in order to warm up the water which was brought in the Calidarium, or hot bathing room (B).

Above the furnaces there are some windows which were opened or closed to keep the temperature in the calidarium constant.

In the period of decline, the thermae were adorned with mosaics and became meeting places.

Walking along, always on the left, you can see the Tepidarium (C) or warm bathing room. Here hot water flowed under the lifted floor and produced steam for the sauna of the owner and of his important guests.

Through a big window you can see the Massage Room (D) with a mosaic floor depicting unction scenes; on this floor there are evident signs of a restoration made during the Byzantine age.

Then, you enter the Frigidarium (E) or cold bathing room. It is an octagonal room with apses used as dressing rooms, and with two swimming pools (F), on the opposite sides of the room, supplied by the acqueduct seen at the entrance.

Here you can see the first mosaic floor representing a marine subject, with fishing Cupids, Nereids, Tritons, sea lions.

Going out, you arrive at the Courtyard (2A) before the entrance of the Villa. Here there are Greek columns (some of them are original, but most of them are copies) crowned by Ionic capitals.

Partial view of the thermal complex.

Praefurnia. *Note the terracotta pipes which had the function of preventing the wall's cracking when the fire in the fireplace was lit in order to heat the water for the Calidarium, or hot-bath room.*

Oiling room. *The mosaic figures represent servant adepts at massage and post-bath oiling.*

Massage room. *Servants massaging their master.*

Frigidarium or cold-bath room. *The scene of the large mosaic is typically aquatic, in it are portrayed Cupid and angels and mythological figures* such as Nereids, Tritons and Sea-lions. Following two details of the cold-bath room.

In the centre there was a fountain. Since the floor converged towards the centre, this fountain collected water which, afterwards, flowed to the semicircular Great Latrine, under the courtyard.

A small canal can be seen which descends a sort of public urinal, as one might call it. Here they performed the «small rite» of urinating.

The seats were arranged in a semi-circle against the walls. They were all marble, and have now been lost. However, in order to have a better idea of how they once were, we will later have the opportunity to see a reconstruction in the ladies' restroom.

Moreover, on your right or in front of you there is the main entrance, with three openings, of which the central opening is the widest one. It is a monumental entrance thant has been the subject of studies made by several archaeologists and historian to discover the patron and the owner of the Villa. Prof. Gentili thought that the entrance, closed with an arch, represented a little Arco di Trionfo (Triumphal Arch), and he inferred that only a high-rank person, the emperor Maximia-

nus Herculeus (1), could have had it built in order to maintain an emotional bond with Rome.

The hypothesis that the patron was the emperor is now unacceptable, and the scholars try to make theses and hypotheses but always with no grounds.

By two steps, you enter the house. You cannot walk on the floor and you are compelled to go up some stairways and look at the mosaics floors of the rooms from above.

The first room is the Aditus or entrance. The mosaic floor represents some people carrying candelabra and small branches of laurel and greeting their owner and other arriving guests.

This room leads you the rectangular Peristyle (38 mt. long and 18 mt. wide) surrounded by Greek columns crowned by Corinthian capitals. The beauty of this Peristyle can be found only in «extraordinary buildings and it is hardly surpassed by the courtyards of the House of Faunus in Pompei, of the Domus Augustana of the Palatino in the Piazza d'Oro and of the Courtyard of the Villa Adriana Library in Tivoli or of the Mega 15

The large latrine.

Corinthain capital on top of one of the peristyle's Greek columns.

Palation in Costantinople» (2).

In the centre there is a nice fountain with a statue and a garden around.

The mosaic floor of the corridor is composed of medallions representing heads of wild and domestic animals.

Leaves of ivy and birds, adorn the inner corners of the single panels. The mosaics is well preserved, the representation is very bright.

Going down an iron stairway, on your left, you can see another latrine equipped with a rectangular bidet. The mosaic floor, with a white background represents animals.

Going on, you visit the Gymnasium or gymnastic hall, the last room of the thermal area. The mosaic depicts the Roma Circus Maximus with chariots of different colours, the colours of the four traditional teams.

The obelisk represented in the centre of this room has given the scholars some problems of interpretation. In fact, according to some hypotheses pointed to the study of the top of those

strange obelisk, some scholars have thought that in this Villa Claudius Mamertinus could have dwelled (3).

Leaving the Gymnasium you pass through a little vestibulo (8A) with a mosaic floor depicting a family and two servant-maids, carrying some boxes with oinments, who are going to the thermae.

Some have thought that the family here depicted might be the imperial family, that is the empress Eutropia and her two sons, Massentius and Fausta, or the family of the Consulares Proculus Populonius (4), that is his wife Adelphia and his sons Proculus and Aradius Rufinis.

So you have finished the visit of the first area and can go on with the second area, the one of the guest-rooms.

Here on the second level we find both geometric and figurative mosaics. The difference lies in the public part, with figurative mosaics, and the private part, with geometric mosaics, of the Villa.

For some scholars the entire complex of mo-

Entrance hall. The mosaic portrays people welcoming their master or expected illustrations guests, with chandelier and lauriel leaves.

saic floors represents man's continuous search for «Roman happiness».

The first room, with a merely geometric mosaic floor, was destroyed during the Arabian domination to build a kiln for the firing of ceramics.

The Arabs inhabited the Villa after the Romans, and made it into their fort, or «hamlet».

Today the term «hamlet» refers only to the farmhouse complex.

Then, you arrive at a room known as the «Ballroom». The mosaic depicts dance scenes, or rather an event of Roman history: «The Rape of the Sabines».

Going on you find two other wonderful rooms: the room of the «Seasons» and that of the «Fishing». The next room is the Diaeta or the living-room of the «Small Hunt», where you can admire some hunting episodes carried out, probably, in the surroundings of the Villa.

Analysing the mosaic you can see: at the centre the sacrifice to Diana, goddes of the hunt; the picnic under a red cloth the scene of the wild boar and the capture of the stag.

After this wonderful room, you go on with the visit of the corridor of the «Great Hunt», about 60 mt long, dedicated to Africa and Armenia. In it you can see hunting scenes carried out in those regions.

On the southern part of the corridor, the floor has got a depression caused by the pressure on the argillaneous ground for the debris accumulated during the centuries.

Fortunately, the tesserae of the mosaic did not break because of their little dimensions.

The «Great Hunt» room divides the II level

red by the Greek sculptor Praxiletes (III-IV century b.C.). The mosaic depicts the poet Orpheus thanking gods and animals moving towards him.

This room is the last one of the second area, and after that you go out to visit the Triclinium — a trilobe room — or dining-room. This very large room was the first one to come to light.

The entire surface of the Villa was in fact covered, and had become countryside.

In 1812 the owner of the estate, who probably wanted to build a well in this area, discovered purely by chance that beneath 8 meters of earth lay mosaic floors.

At the time the periodic digging began, which from the III, with the owner's rooms. We may imagine that while waiting to be received by the owner, who was in the meeting room which can be seen in the middle of the corridor, people came up and down discussing problems of daily life. Because of this, we also call it the corridor

The peristyle. The mosaic floored corridors present a double train of medallions within whose rings figure the heads of wild and domestic animals, ferocious beasts and birds.

of lost steps.

Going on you arrive at the room known as the «Room of the Girls in bikinis».

This room has got two floors, because the present Villa was built on a fairly nice rustic building.

To let the tourists see a part of the mosaic floor below it was a good idea of the archaeologists.

The girls represent the Games: putting the shot, discus throwing, ball game, running.

In the lower part of the floor, on the left, you can see the winner with some servant-maids. Going on you can see the inner aqueduct and the Diaeta (living-room) of Orpheus. Here you can admire a very beautiful statue of Lycian Apollo. This statue is a roman copy of the one sculptu-

The peristyle. A wide rectangular quadrangle in whose central courtyard is a large fountain adorned with a statue surrounded by a garden.

The latrine. Mosaic with animal figures.

The gymnasium. The mosaic portrays a competition at Rome's Circus Maximus with quadrigas. Here the winner is awarded a victory palm by a togaed magistrate.

The Gymnasium. Portrait of the temples dedicated to the goddes Roma and to Jove.

The small entrance hall. A mother accompanies her children to the Thermae. At the sides are two maidservants with everything necessary for the bath. To the right, a particular of the mosaic.

The guest room. Geometric floor designs.

Ball room. Particular of a young female dancer whose silk veil flies around, while she dances. Ball room. Particular of the mosaiced flooring. The mosaic could simulate the Sabine rat.

Rooms of the seasons. In the rings of the geometric squares are portrayed: Spring, a slender bust of a woman; Summer, a strong youth with ears of com *on his head; Autumn, a fained girl with the body doubled up; Winter, a bust of a man with his head crowned with leaves.*

The guest room. Mosaic floor with geometric designs. Various species of birds and fish are portrayed in the rings.

Fishing room. The mosaic portrays a fishing scene. Moments and methods of fishing in a sea rich in fish, in which the cupid angels work with elan and vitality.

Mounted horsemen push the deer into the net.

The small-game hunting room. In the centre of the scene a propitiatory sacrifice to Diana the huntress takes place.

A wild bear is about to be beaten to death after having put an unfortunate hunter in difficulty.

The fallen bear is tied and carried on the shoulders of two hunters.

A mounted huntsman about to strike a have.

31

On the left: Small-game hunting room. A picnic scene: under a red drape and under the shadow of the trees, the hunters grant themselves a well-deserved rest and a luxurious meal based on game.

Corridor of the «big-game hunting»: The whole portrays a big-game beating: from the chase of the hunters, to the capture of the wild beasts and other kinds of animals.

The hunters have prepared the bait for the wild beasts' capture.

Various moments of the big-game hunting are portrayed with such a grace and expressive elegance, as to render more efficacious the polychromicity of the mosaic stones, creating a sensation of vivacity and movement in the portrayed scenes.

To the top right, is the meaning-ful figure of a wing gryphon, holding a man, the destroyer of nature, in a cage in its claws. To the bottom, a tiger showing its maternal love prepares itself to go to the aid of its abandoned cub.

On the following page: A sailing ship prepares to load. A goat is being dragged aboard.

37

A virtually loaded boat gets ready to leave.

The scene represents the personification of Africa, with an elephant, a tiger and a phoenix in its natural habitat.

in 1952 brought to light this magnificent complex you are viewing.

The mosaics depist the «Labours of Hercules».

In the exedrae, in front of the entrance you can see the «Battle between Gods and Giants»; on the left, the «Apotheosis of Hercules»; on the right is represented the «Legend of Lycurgus and Ambrosia», that is the myth that tells the metamorphosis of Ambrosia into wine caused by Apollo, to prevent Lycurgus from killing Ambrosia.

Going out, in front of you there is the Xistus, the open space where probably the owner walked together with his guests after a sumptuous dinner.

On hot days under the shelter of tents.

To the left and right we can see the kitchens where meals were prepared.

When you finish this visit, there is nothing else to see but the last area, that is the family quarters, the rooms of the wife, of the two sons, of the owner and, last but not least, the alcove.

But before moving on to visit the various rooms, we must say that the surrounding wall, which can be seen by looking towards the mountain, saved the villa from total distruction. The wall acted as a barrier against the flood that came from up the mountain, making the water, mixed with every sort of refuse, flow past smoothly.

By an iron stairway you enter the Lady's room. The bed was put in the exedra and in front of it there was an ornamental fountain, where it is possible that the maids served their Domina (The Lady). The mosaic of this room represents the myth of Arion.

Arion is going to be killed by the crew of his ship, who intended to steal his riches, so Jupiter sends a dolphin in order to save him; the poet, therefore, thanks the god playing his lyre while sitting on the dolphin.

Both on the right and on the left of this room there are the ones of her sons. The mosaics represent the Circus Maximus in miniature with only domestic animals, and the myth of Eros and Pan.

Room of the «Girls in Bikinis». The scene is divided in two horizontal sections: the upper part figuring weight-lifting, discus-throwing and racing scenes; the lower, from the left, a handball game, a girl with a victory palm who is putting a crown, and finally the awards granted by a young maiden in a gold cloak, who is preparing to give the crown and the palm to the other girl who holds in her left hand the wheel of the Cistercian games.

41

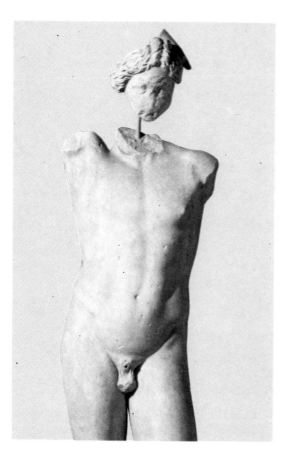

Eros, god of Love; Pan, god of the mountains, of the herds. A battle is about to be fought between them. The winner will have the two purses, which can be seen under the table, as his prize. On the purses are shown Roman numerals: these indicate the amount of money in each.

Going outside you can visit the private latrine, and the owner's room in which is represented the myth of Ulysses and Polyphemus. The Cyclop is strangely depicted with three eyes, and this might be explained with the fact that the artist considered the double nature of Polyphemus, as man and monster.

The scene takes place in a cave of the volcano Aetna. We can see Ulysses, who is giving the cyclops a cup of wine with opium to make him

Room of the Orpheus journey. On the left is a beautiful portray of Apollo Lyceus. The mosaiced scene on the floor, portrays the sublime legend of the mild singer, who with the sweet sound of his zither manages to enchant trees and animals, which run with the sublime music throged around him as enchanted spectators.

On the right, the god Apollo crowns Hercules head with laurel in honour of his victorious tasks.

Here one can admire the five giants afflicted by a strong pain in the act of tearing out the deadly darts cast by the Hero.

drunk and then blind him, with the burning point of a tree trunk, and flee with his companions clinging to the bellies of the animals.

On the left you can see the alcove with a central medallion depicting the «Erotic Scene». This scene is very delicate, not pornographic, and depicts two youths embracing each other.

With this last room you have visited the noble part of the Villa, the so-called Domus; bust must still be brought to light the dépendances and something else that might give us more precise information concerning the patron of this wonderful monument.

To the left is Ambrosia who has already begun her metamorphosis into a vine. At top, Lycurgus in the act of hitting the Bacchante Ambrosia with berries whilst her metamorphosis is taking place. Finally, a horse's head and a particular of the scene of the tasks of Hercules.

The exedra porticoes of the corridor of the big game hunt. The scene of the mosaic floor portrays winged Cupids, intent on fishing and other playing amongst the waves and with the fish and aquatic animals, while at the bottom of the scene there are lively buildings linked to each other by long porticoes.

In a boat two Cupids are practising every type of fishing in the fish-filled sea, using harpoon, hands or net: the bounty is rich.

The room of Airone. To the right, the poet Airone appears among the waves mounted on a dolphin, playing the zither, as he is circled by sea monsters from the sea in the semblance of gryphons, tigers, panthers, wolves, lions and bully on backs of which are riding pretty Cupids. Naiads, Water-nymphs, with elegant feminity, fill the mithological scene, completing it.

The room of Airone. Naiads with graceful and elegant feminity, sea monsters in the semblance of animals, on whose backs are riding Cupids, encircle the mythological figure of Airone. Particulars of the mosaic scene dedicated to the poet Airone.

The room of the children. The mosaic portrays the Circus Maximus in miniature. A contest is in progress in the arena, with four chariots pulled by pairs of large domestic animals, web-footed and other flying creatures, driven by young boys.

Hall of the choirs and the artists. The mosaic portrays two girls at the sides of a tree dominated — upon which by the ivy leaf, symbol of the Emperor Maximinian Hercules.

The room with the myth of Eros and Pan. At the centre of the floor scene, one can admire the combat between the goathooved and the winged Eros. Between the two is a victory palm. To the left of Pan, is the arbitre and to the right of Eros the spectators.

The children's room. The mosaic portrays a humorous hunting scene, which has young boys as its main protagonists. The particular shows a have which is pierced.

Children's room. **The mosaics depict an amusing hunting scene which features a group of children: the cock chases and pecks at the child who has fallen; the duckling writhes after having been caught in a trap. Floral compositions frame the scene. The mosaic depicting a boy bearing a staff, at the end of which are two baskets of roses, are in excellent condition.**

57

The private latrine. The master's room portrays the homeric scene of the myth of Odysseus and Polyphemus. Polyphemus sat inside a cave surrounded by sheep and goats, is preparing to receive a cup full of wine from the astute Odysseus.

The cubicle of the erotic scene. The mosaiced floor of this room is in an optimum state of conservation. The scene is a geometric composition which extends over the whole surface with perfect harmony.

Aidone

Rises in the Erei mountains to 850 m above sea level. The territory is very great and projects onto the plane of Catania, sheltered by thick woods. Woods which are difficult to find in Sicily, not for the interminable number of plants but rather for their rarity. The houses climb up a slope and from the windows or terraces it is possible to overwiev virtually the whole of Sicily. A wonderful and unimaginable countryside awaits anyone who looks from the Belvedere (panoramic viewpoint) of Aidone's Villa Comunale.

The origins of Aidone are last in time. It is said that the original nucleus of the first inhabitants comes from the neighbouring city of Morgantina, abandoned in the Roman period towards the end of the first century B.C. For nearly a thousand years, Aidone did not make history, or, better, there were no historical events which have made known the splendor and the importance that Morgantina had had, even through the names of some of the contrades or quarters, some dialectal expressions, the remains of the Arab architecture in the church of Saint Anthony testify that Aidone, like the rest of Sicily, was subjected to the Arab invasion.

The real history of Aidone begins with Ruggero the Norman towards the second half of the 11th century. With the Norman, domination town planning material is outlined, and some monuments arise, such as the Castle, the Church of Sainty Leon, the Church of St. Maria la Cava, and the Monastery of St. Michael. Unfortunately the earthquake of 1693 deprovcd these monuments of their original Mediaeval Architecture.

The Basilica of St. Leon. Of the Mediaeval Era, the Basilica of St. Leon was built in 1090 using as its foundations, megalithic stones from the Citadel, where a thousand years before rose Morgantine. The Basilica is dedicated to Pope Leon II, who was of Aidonese origin, even through his was a brief pontificate.

The principal characteristic is the baroque portal of sand stone bordered by two stepped, projecting columns culminating in Corinthian capitals.

The Basilica of St. Leon is one of Aidone's most ancient monuments: it was from this very Basilica that the building of houses had its origin.

The Church of Saint Dominic is an example of the figurative Sicilian culture of the 1400 s; it was built in 1419 by the Dominican Vincenzo Pistoia. The principle characteristic of the building is the «diamond point» decorative motif, a style brought to Sicily by the Spaniards.

In the 1600s the building was restructured with baroque decorative elements in mountain sandstone from a nearly quary. The portal is adorned with beautiful sculptures with pilaster strips which culminate in Corinthian capitals and angels heads.

The corners of this building end in a depressed tympanum with strongly projecting horizontal corners under which a frieze, emphasized by metope and clover leaves, puts into evidence the artists' inspiration who, decorating the church of Saint Dominic, was thinking of a Doric temple.

The Church of Saint Anthony is the oldest building of the Aidonese community. Very probably it was a religious building, constructed by the Arabs and successively remodellated in the Roman Era.

In the Middle Ages the Church was reconstructed on a basilican plan with trifolium architecture and dedicated to Christianity. The Normans closed the original narrow door and the Southern windows, and built another entrance to the West in the Gothic style with an ogival arch in alternating hewn stones, white and black, sandstone and white stone from Comiso.

The bell-tower dates from the 1600s and was built by the Normans with two levels of single windows at the four sides and culminating in a spire covered in spherical elements multicoloured ceramics.

The Mother Church was built before the year 1000 in honour of the glorious martyr Saint Lawrence, Patron of Aidone.

The building has a perfectly rectangular shape, without lateral projections, and due to its structure, dominated by ideas of calm and serenity, resembles and old pagan temple destined, following the Birth of Christianity, to Catholicism.

The bell-tower and the four chapels placed laterally to the building, two to the right and two to the left, are from a more recent Era.

Destroyed by the earthquake of 1963, its restoration is being carried out replacing the old material in the principle facade in order not to

Ruins of the 11th century Saracen Castle, destroyed by an earthquake in 1693.

The Church of St. Dominic (1419) with a diamond point façade.

by the Vaccaro brothers of Caltagirone, the picture of the Assumption of the 1700s by an unknown artist, the picture of the Indulgence of the Portiuncola (place where St. Francis of Assisi was born) by an unknown artist of the 1600s, the picture of the Immaculate Mary by an unknown artist of the 1700s, the Stations of the Cross by an unknown artist of the 1800s, and finally the Crucifix, one of the most important pieces, sculpted by Brother Umile Pintorno of Petralia. Annexed to the Church one can visit the ex-monastery of the Reformed Fathers or the Observants of Saint Anna, of which remains the cloister with arches outlines by terracotta bricks on the splender doric columns.

The Catle of the *Gresti* is an ancient building of the Norman Era which rises on the summit of a rock in the middle of bood valley, in the centre of the triangle formed by Aidone, Raddusa and Valguarnera. It is possible to reach it easily, travelling along the SS 288 as far as Raddusa and continuing along the local road which, only partially asphalted, runs along the River Gorralunga through wonderful countryside.

sully the artistic main door.

Conserved in the Church are the two statues belonging to St. Catherine's Church, the splendid canvas depicting the martyrdom of St. Lawrence and the Holy Relic of a bone of Saint Levita's arm. Round and unplintered, five fingers long it is encased in a silver arm. The authenticity of the relic is justified by a document in a sealed parchement and seen by many diocesan bishops; the beloved Martyr and Patron of the city has his feast-day on the 10th of August.

The Church of Saint Maria la Cava was founded in 1134 by Adelasia, niece of Count Ruggero the Norman. Annexed to the Church there is the bell-tower whose ogival door, today walled up, positioned at the base surrounds the original destination of the building which was that of a Norman tower. In 1400 the tower was destroyed and rebuilt in Gothic-Catalan style of which there remains a trace in the single window of the bell-tower with an ongival arch in white stone.

This building encloses within itself three great artistic eras which do nothing but enhance its great effect. The Church, adorned inside with frescoes by Clelia Argentati, is today the Sanctuary of St. Philip the Apostle and target of pilgrimage for the Saint's feast day which is on the 1st of May.

The Church of Saint Anna has its origins in the 1600s even through influences dating back to the Arab period, which can be seen in the external wall is, in fact, an extension of the ancient masque which later, with the coming of the Normans, was transformed into a Christian Church. The interior of the Church is in the form of an aisle and holds many works of art among which are, the picture of Saint Francis of Paola of 1865

Morgantina

Is a grandiose Hellenized-Sicilian city which existed from the 10th century B.C. Its remains are found in the region of Serra Orlando, four kms from Aidone and are reachable by using the SS 228 (the n. of a national road). It was brought to light in 1955, thanks to Princeton University, and was considered, rightly, the most important archeological discovery made in Sicily in the 20th century.

A comparison to Pompei is not daring. In fact around 30 B.C. the city of Morgantina was misteriously abandoned, and covered with a layer of dust and ashes. It has been thus preserved until out time as it was in the days of its great splendor.

The excavations. The most important, and most noted, part of the city, on which the excavations have been concentrated, is central part. Two sectors have so far been uncovered; one public and one private. The first, completely open to the public comprises the Agora and its public buildings. The second, known as the Levant residential quarter, comprises three private buildings, and divertly borders the Agora. A second far large residential quarter is found on the little hill to the West of the Agora (the Ponente or Western residential quarter) and comprises six clusters of houses on which only three are completely excavated.

THE AGORA

The Agora is divided in two sections, at different levels. The high part, to the North-West, is slightly trapezoidal shaped, surrounded on three sides by long, covered squares, without colonnades. The lower part, separated from the first by a large stairway, is, contrarily, a grouping of Public buildings: the Theatre, Granary, Sanctuary and the Furnace.

The Gymnasium seat of learning and sporting activities; the East-Portico, a seat of the administration of the people courts; the perypatetic school and place of business encounters; Tabernae with workshops at the back, built in the Hellenistic Era; Bouleuteryon, the seat of the city Senate; the Monumental Fountain with two pools, built in the second half of the 11th century B.C. and dedicated to the Nymphs; Macellum a covered markct comparable to a modern supermarket; the trapezoidal flight of stairs with 14 steps It is thought to identify the Ekklesiasterion in it, the seat of the People's assembly, more recently, a cultural place linked to the Sanctuary of the Divinity Ctonie, found below it.

The theatre. The theatre occupies the South-Western side of the lower Agora. Three essential components area clearly distinguishable in it: 1) the Cavea or Tribune; for public use, comprising 15 orders of steps subdivided into six sectors and help up by walls provided with internal einforcements: it could hold over 1.000 spectators; 2) the Orchestra, space reserved for the movement of the Chorus, semicircular in shape and immediately below the Cavea; 3) the Scena for the actors and separated from the rest of the front structure by two entrance gangways (Parodoi).

To the East by the theatre, and in strict relation to it, rises a Sanctuary dedicated to Demeter and Kore, the two divine protectors of the city and propitiators of good harvests. It represents one of the principle Sanctuaries found at Morgantine. **The Public Granary.** It has been related

to the Lex Hieronica, promulgated by Hieronus II, in virtue of which Morgantina payed a tenth of its wheath harvest to Syracuse, receiving in exchange protection and technical assistance in the construction of its public buildings.

The Furnace. In the shape of a broad tunnel, divided by arches, is visible in the South-Eastern corner of the Agora. It produces Terracotta products destined for the building trade.

Prytaneion, place of the Supreme Magistrate, is the first building, one meets on entering the street which joins the Agora to the Levant residential quarter. It is a large house endowed with a central peristyle, collonaded on three sides, onto which opens a series of rooms.

House of the Doric Capital. The entrance was to the West. Through a corridor, one entered the peristyle, around which the various rooms are arranged. The central courtyard, surrounded by eight columns of stuccoed ringed bricks, had the

5

Morgantina:
1. Entrance to the excavations.
2. Gymnasium.
3. Hellenistic shops.
4. Macellum
5. Theatre.

function of collecting rainwater conducting it to the two cisterns. The East side of the habitation is occupied by three large rooms; the most southerly, the smallest, has a beautiful floor of *«beaten white»* with polychromatic mosaic stones, and remains of basic wall decorations. In the North comes is a group of rooms to access to which one gains from a square hall, with a pressed terracotta floor beautifully decorated with meanders in white mosaic stones. The South side was occupied by service rooms. One of the rooms which opens onto the peristyle has a beautiful pressed terracotta floor with an inscription in Greek: «Welcome».

The House of Ganymede. So called because of the subject depicted on a fine mosaic floor. The large central peristyle measures 17 metres and comprises 16 columns. Below it is a large cistern, while a second is in the South-West corner. The most important rooms were on the North-East side, facing the sunnier slope to the South-West: here there was also a second floor, as the collapse of structures pertinent to it shows. Two small rooms open onto the peristyle. In one of these one finds the famous mosaic of Ganymede's rat, and is one of the oldest examples of the Hellenistic technique in mosaic stones.

THE ARCHEOLOGICAL MUSEUM

It was opened in 1984 and is sited in a seventeenth century Capuchin Monastery, restructured for the purpose. We can, therefore, speak of one Museum within another. The entrance is represented by what was the Monastery's Church, and in this, which also acts as a conference hall, it is possible to observe the head of Brother Umile of Petralia's, «Ecce Homo», with the three facial expressions dependent on which side one is admiring; the High Altar in guilded wood, the canvasses, of which the central one represents the Nativity; the Statues of Saint Felix, Saint Antony and Saint Joseph; the little 18th Century terracotta Madonna. The founds kept at the Museum have been arranged in chronological and topographical order, they infact refer to three digging areas (see table 1) and to three corresponding periods.

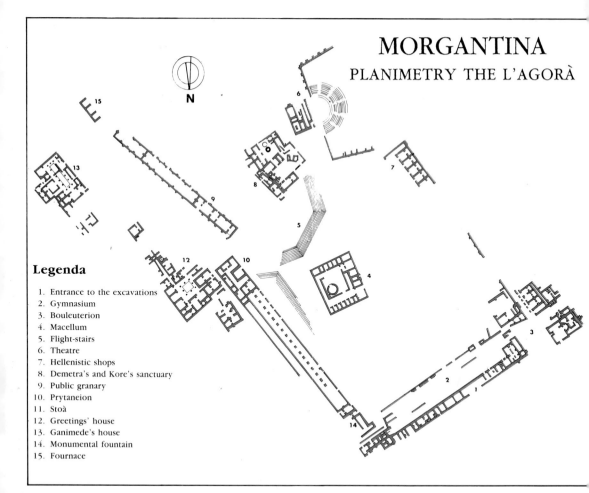

MORGANTINA
PLANIMETRY THE L'AGORÀ

N

Legenda

1. Entrance to the excavations
2. Gymnasium
3. Bouleuterion
4. Macellum
5. Flight-stairs
6. Theatre
7. Hellenistic shops
8. Demetra's and Kore's sanctuary
9. Public granary
10. Prytaneion
11. Stoà
12. Greetings' house
13. Ganimede's house
14. Monumental fountain
15. Fournace

CONTENTS

Art Director:
Federico Frassinetti

Photography:
Ascanio Ascani - Misano (Fo)
Raimondo Marino

Editions **ITALCARDS** bologna - italy

AUTHOR'S NOTES

(1) **G. Vinicio Gentili**, La Villa Imperiale di Piazza Armerina. *Istituto Poligrafico dello Stato.*
(2) **Biagio Pace**, *in* «I Mosaici di Piazza Armerina». *Ed. Tipografia Castaldi, Roma, pp. 30-31, luglio 1955.*
(3) **Antonio Ragona**, *in* «L'Obelisco di Costanzo II e la datazione dei Mosaici di Piazza Armerina». *Caltagirone 1966.*
(4) **A. Carandini, A. Ricci, M. De Vos**, Filosofiana. La Villa di Piazza Armerina. *Ed. S.F. Flaccovio, Palermo 1982.*

LA FOTOMETALGRAFICA EMILIANA SPA
San Lazzaro di Savena - Bologna